GIRL TALK

CARDS AND GIFTS

Style Secrets for Girls

STEPHANIE TURNBULL

A+

Smart Apple Media

Published by Smart Apple Media, an imprint of Black Rabbit Books
P.O. Box 3263, Mankato, Minnesota 56002
www.blackrabbitbooks.com

Library of Congress Cataloging-in-Publication Data

Turnbull, Stephanie.
Cards and gifts : style secrets for girls / by Stephanie
Turnbull.
p. cm.—(Girl Talk)
Summary: "A fun magazine-like book for preteen and
teen girls on crafty ways to make and present gifts. Includes
information on materials that work best and step-by-step instructions to create cards, envelopes, photo frames,
cookies, and other treats for girls"—Provided by publisher.
Audience: Grades 4-6.
Includes index.
ISBN 978-1-59920-944-9 (library binding)—ISBN 978-1-62588-995-9 (ebook)
1. Handicraft for girls—Juvenile literature. 2. Greeting cards—Juvenile literature. I. Title.
TT171.T874 2014
745.594'1—dc23
                    2012051546

Created by Appleseed Editions Ltd
Designed and illustrated by Guy Callaby
Edited by Mary-Jane Wilkins

Picture credits
t = top, b = bottom, l = left, r = right, c = center
title page Ermolaev Alexander/Shutterstock; page 2t Hong Vo, b Tina Rencelj/both Shutterstock; 3 Rigamondis/
Shutterstock; 4t Guy Callaby, l iStockphoto/Thinkstock, b Victorian Traditions/Shutterstock; 5c onstik/
Shutterstock, b Hemera/Thinkstock; 6t evanrin20, c papers: paper under text Pigdevil Photo, orange Malgorzata
Kistryn, hand-made with pink KsushaArt, hand-made with green lobster20, hand-made with beige akiyoko, torn
paper roll Elnur/all Shutterstock; 7 crocuses ultimathule, pink flower Vilor, heart/cloud kearia, gold cake zphoto/all
Shutterstock; shoes: pink ski boots and red shoe/striped tights both iStockphoto/Thinkstock, pink and black shoes/
tights and pink soft boots Hemera/Thinkstock, red stilettos, girl holding pink shoe, open sandals all
iStockphoto/Thinkstock, coloured shapes Janaka Dharmasena/Shutterstock; 8t iStockphoto/
Thinkstock; 10t shooarts/Shutterstock; 11b kanate/Shutterstock; 12t artforyou, bows: Liliya
Kulianionak, b Tom Biegalski/all Shutterstock; 14t Terrie L. Zeller, l bonchan, fabric under text s74/
all Shutterstock; 15 NoName Photo/Shutterstock; 16 frames: letters/numbers Tomas Jasinskis,
beaded Linn Currie, cinnamon thumb, pink flower CABO, b shy/all Shutterstock; 17 oliveromg/
Shutterstock; 18t JohnKwan, c R. MACKAY PHOTOGRAPHY, LLC, b Skazka Graz/all Shutterstock;
19tl (t to b) Claudio Baldini, Nattika, Harm Kruyshaar, r stockcreations/all Shutterstock; 20t Ingrid
Balabanova/Shutterstock; 22 Vanessa Nel/Shutterstock; 23 FLariviere/Shutterstock; 24l Yuttasak
Jannarong, r Lisa F. Young/both Shutterstock; 25t Rebecca Sheehan, b getIT/both Shutterstock; 26t
Gorilla, herbs: chives petratlu, basil martiapunts, coriander Snowbelle, rosemary Dionisvera, mint
fotohunter, r joyfuldesigns/all Shutterstock; 27 Elnur/Shutterstock; 28t Darrin Henry, l sniegirova
mariia, bc Phiseksit, br Reika/all Shutterstock; 30Picsfive/Shutterstock; 31 photosyn/Shutterstock;
32 DenisNata/Shutterstock

Front cover: DenisNata/Shutterstock

Printed in the United States at Corporate Graphics in North Mankato, Minnesota.
PO DAD5005
052013

9 8 7 6 5 4 3 2 1

Contents

Personal Touches

You can buy all kinds of cards and gifts, but it's far more fun to make your own. Personally-designed presents and hand-crafted cards are much more special than anything in stores—and a lot cheaper, too!

Start Giving

There are so many reasons to make things for your friends or family. Perhaps you need to say happy birthday, thank you, congratulations, sorry, or get well soon. Maybe you just want to say hello! Be thoughtful—it could make someone's day.

Fun Card Facts

Handmade paper greeting cards date back to the early 1400s.

Valentine's Day cards became popular in the 1800s. They were often made with lace and ribbons.

Send cards to your BFFs on Friendship Day? It is the first Sunday in August. And don't forget Sweetest Day on the third Saturday in October!

Think Crafty

The crafts in this book use lots of everyday materials, so start saving useful items, such as pieces of colored cards, ribbons, beads, buttons, and sequins. You'll also need good scissors and a glue stick or white craft or school glue.

Try to be organized and lay out everything you need before starting a craft project.

Before You Begin

Think about who your card or gift is for, what they like, and the occasion. Does the person need a treat to cheer them up, a practical present they can use, or something to make them laugh? Choose themes, colors, and styles that suit them, not you.

Always work carefully and neatly to avoid making mistakes.

Pssst... Hot Tip!

Look out for these tips throughout the book. They give you extra ideas, tricks, and advice on how to create fantastic cards and gifts.

Clever Collage

Handmade cards often look tricky to make, but don't despair if you're not a gifted artist! Start with these quick and easy **collage** techniques, and you'll soon be creating professional-looking cards.

Style Secrets

Use good-quality cardstock or paper, and make sure you cut and fold it neatly. Before adding a picture, glue down a smaller panel of cardstock in a contrasting color. **Mount** your image on this panel to focus attention on it.

Pssst... Clear a large space to work at, and have a trash can nearby for scraps, otherwise you'll end up with a big mess!

Think Smart

Who says you have to design your own shapes for a collage? Cut eye-catching images from old greeting cards and glue them down to create new designs. Simple cards are often effective, so sometimes just one image is enough.

Magazine Montages

Photomontage cards are fun to make. Choose a theme—for example, a fashion-forward friend might like a montage of shoes, clothes, and accessories. Cut out pictures from old magazines and cover your card with them.

Overlap a few pictures and let some run off the edge of the central panel.

Experiment with different layouts before gluing anything down.

Simple Shapes

Another collage method is to cut shapes from patterned or shiny wrapping paper. Use cardboard templates or trace objects to make identical shapes.

Leave small gaps between shapes to give a clever mosaic effect.

Make a bunch of paper circles using a hole punch, then turn them into funky patterns.

Eye-Catching Cards

Go beyond flat—make an impact with designs that stand out from the paper. The simplest way of adding depth is to layer shapes, or stick small squares of cardboard behind images to raise them. Here are some more smart ideas.

Up, Up, and Away

Lift the edges of shapes to make them look as if they're about to fly off the card! Draw and cut out a cardboard butterfly template, then use it to make two identical butterflies from colored paper. Make one darker than the other.

This creates a great shadow effect.

Glue down the darker butterfly, then stick the lighter butterfly on top, but only glue the body. Curl up the butterfly's wings a little.

Make more butterflies and add details with crayons or stick sequins on the wings.

Perky Petals

Follow these easy steps to make fantastic 3D flower cards.

1. Make a 4.5 in x 4 in (12 cm x 10 cm) rectangle from colored paper and fold it in half.

2. Fold it in half again.

3. Fold up the top layer to make a triangle, like this.

4. Turn it over, and do the same on the other side.

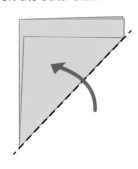

5. Draw a curved line across the triangle to make a petal shape. Cut along it, through all the layers of the paper.

6. Open your finished flower shape.

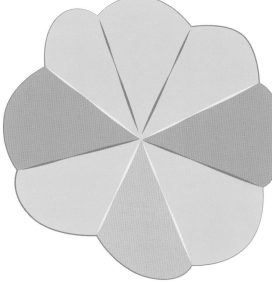

7. Cut out more flowers in different colors, or use wrapping paper, tissue paper, or cellophane. For smaller flowers, draw the curve in step 5 lower. You can also cut more waves to form different petal shapes.

Layer and glue them on your card, with a button in the center of each.

Pssst... Use paper flowers to decorate wrapped presents, too!

Perfect Pop-ups

Give someone a surprise with a neat pop-up picture inside a card! Complicated pop-ups use inventive cutting, folding, and gluing techniques—but these easy methods only take a few minutes.

Ledge Pop-ups

This is the simplest and best way to make a picture stand up.

1. Fold a piece of cardstock in half. At the fold, draw two lines near the center.

2. Cut along the lines and fold over the flap.

3. Unfold the flap, open the card, and push up the flap inside. This makes a neat ledge.

4. Fold a slightly larger piece of cardstock in half to make the outside of the card. Glue the two pieces together.

5. Glue a picture to the front of the ledge, and it will stand up when the card opens. Don't make it too big, or it will show when the card is closed.

Pssst... Cut several ledges to add extra pop-ups. Shorter flaps make smaller ledges.

Silly Mouths

These mouthy pop-ups will make your friends smile.

1. *Make one cut in the middle of a folded card.*

2. *Fold back the edges.*

3. *Unfold the flaps, open the card, and push them inwards.*

4. *Now close the card and press it flat.*

5. *Fold a slightly larger piece of cardstock in half and glue it to the back. Have fun decorating your big open mouth!*

ribbit!

Remember to decorate the outside of the card, too!

Pop-ups were first made in the 13th century.

The art of folding paper is called origami, and comes from Japan.

Paper and Pop-ups

Origami that involves cutting and gluing is called kirigami.

More Materials

Art and craft shops sell beautiful card decorations including fabric flowers, lacy edging, foam stickers, and sparkling gems. They look good, but the cost adds up—instead, design some homemade extras.

Natural Beauty

Dried, pressed leaves, petals, and flowers make delicate decorations for **borders**, corners, or the center of cards. To prepare your blooms and foliage, lay them on a piece of paper inside a heavy, open book. Place another sheet of paper on top, shut the book, and pile more books on top. These pretty embellishments will be ready in a couple of weeks.

Pssst... Don't pick wild flowers! Use plants from your house or garden, and ask permission first.

Beautiful Borders

Try threading ribbon or lace to create an attractive border for a flat invitation or thank you note.

This type of punch tool lets you choose different hole sizes.

1. Cut a rectangle of paper and make eight evenly-spaced holes down each side with a hole punch or craft punch tool.

2. Add four holes along the top and bottom of the card.

If it helps, mark where you want the holes with a pencil first.

Angle the hole punch to make one hole at a time.

3. Thread thin ribbon or lace in and out of the holes. Tie a bow at the top and trim the ends. Glue on a smaller rectangle for your message.

If your bow won't lie flat, glue it in place.

X
Thank
You!!
XXX

Add Some Bling

For fancier borders, why not thread shiny beads on ribbon? Or instead of a bow at the top, hang a small pendant or charm from a forgotten necklace or bracelet. Hunt through old jewelry and see what you can find!

Finishing Touches

Thoughtful finishing touches make homemade cards look special. Think about what to say in your card and use a good pen. If you don't have neat handwriting, print out your message in fancy font instead!

Wavy Edges

Tools such as **pinking shears**, which cut paper with a wiggly edge, are great for giving borders and panels a fun look. Use them to cut fabric or **felt** squares and mount your design on top.

Origami Envelopes

Don't forget an envelope! You may have spare envelopes of the right size, but making your own is a great finishing touch. Use this easy origami method to make a wrapping paper envelope that fits perfectly.

1. Cut a piece of paper roughly three times as wide as your card and a little less than an inch (2 cm) longer at each end.

Please come to my...

2. *Fold the paper in half lengthwise, then unfold it.*

3. *Fold the top corners into the fold to make a triangle. This is the flap.*

4. *Place your card under the center of the flap and fold in each edge over the card.*

Keep these edges the same width all the way down.

lease con my...

5. *Fold the bottom of the paper up over the card. Fold in any extra paper so this section lines up with the edge of the card.*

6. *Secure the flap with a sticker or glued-on decoration, such as a button or plastic gem.*

Pssst… Be inventive and make envelopes from wallpaper, old maps, or even tin foil.

Envelope Extras
If you aren't mailing your envelope, add decorations, such as ribbon, gift bows, or paper cutouts. There's no reason the envelope shouldn't be as creative as the card inside!

Fab Photo Gifts

Photos make the perfect personalized gift – especially if they're in a fantastic frame! Here are some inventive ways to display treasured photographs of family, friends, or pets.

Fast Frames

Make a simple frame by gluing a photo to a larger piece of thick cardboard, then glue overlapping paper around it. Be sure to cover all the cardboard and the edges of the photo.

Pssst... Why not liven up a plain wooden picture frame with a collage, **acrylic paints,** or even dabs of shiny nail polish?

More Frame Fun

Make a traditional photo frame and decorate it any way you want.

1. Cut two pieces of cardstock bigger than your photo. Place the photo in the middle of one piece and draw around it.

2. Draw a slightly smaller shape inside the first lines. Cut around these inner lines.

3. Decorate the frame with a creative collage using beads, buttons, sequins, feathers, or other craft supplies.

Pick materials and designs that suit the picture— for example, sand and shells for a day at the beach or bone shapes for your pet dog.

Try drawing swirls and shapes on the back, then rest the frame on a pile of magazines and prick along the lines with a thick, blunt needle. Press down hard.

Turn over the frame and you have a delicate **embossed** design.

4. Tape your photo, face down, to the back of the frame. Glue the second piece of cardstock to the back.

5. Tape on ribbon to hang the frame, or glue on a magnet to turn it into a fun fridge magnet.

Sweet Treats

Homemade goodies are an ideal gift for someone with a sweet tooth, especially if you present them attractively. Start with this easy recipe to create tantalizing **truffles** without doing any cooking!

Before You Start

When making edible gifts think about what the person likes and whether they have a food **allergy** or **intolerance**. Is your workspace clean and have you washed your hands? Store food properly and don't nibble ingredients as you go!

Coconut Truffles

These bite-sized truffles are fun to decorate. Experiment with cake decorations such as sprinkles and edible glitter, or try grated chocolate or chopped nuts.

You will need:

♥ 2 c. (475 mL) powdered sugar
♥ 14 oz (400 g) can condensed milk
♥ 2½ c. (600 mL) shredded coconut
♥ fine cake decorations

1. Mix the powdered sugar and half of the condensed milk in a large bowl. Stir in the coconut.

2. Using clean hands, mold the mixture into one big, sticky lump, then break off small pieces and roll them into balls.

3. *Put the rest of the condensed milk in a bowl next to plates with the decorations. Dip each ball in the condensed milk so it's sticky, then roll it in one of the decorations.*

4. *Set the balls on a large plate or tray, cover with cling wrap, and put in the fridge for a few hours to harden.*

5. *Put the truffles in mini cupcake liners. Arrange them in an attractive box or basket lined with tissue paper and decorated with gift wrap, bows, or plastic gems.*

Turn to page 29 to find out how to make an origami gift box.

Pssst... *To give your truffles even more color, divide the mixture into several sections in step 2 and* **knead** *a few drops of food coloring into each.*

Sweet Stuff

Truffles can be made of cream, chocolate, fudge, marshmallow, and other sweet ingredients.

Petits fours are dainty cookies, cakes, or pastries that can be served for dessert.

Hot chocolate was originally a bitter-tasting drink from Mexico and South America. It was later sweetened with sugar and milk.

Clever Cookies

Freshly-baked cookies smell and taste delicious. Here are two useful recipes you can adapt to create your own versions. Be careful near hot stoves and ovens, and ask an adult to help.

Chocolate Crunches

Turn plain cookies into crunchy chocolate treats! Try adding chopped nuts, dried fruit, or seeds.

You will need:

- ♥ 25 shortbread cookies
- ♥ ½ c. (120 mL) butter
- ♥ 3 Tbsp (45 mL) corn syrup
- ♥ 2 Tbsp (30 mL) cocoa powder
- ♥ ¼ c. (60 mL) raisins
- ♥ 1 c. (250 mL) chocolate chips

1. Put the cookies in a plastic bag and crush them with your hands or a rolling pin.

2. Melt the butter in a large pan over a gentle heat, then mix in the syrup, cocoa powder and raisins. Remove from the heat and stir in the cookie crumbs.

3. Spoon the mixture into a pan lined with parchment paper. Spread and press down with the back of a metal spoon.

4. Microwave the chocolate chips for 30 seconds, stir, then heat for another 30 seconds until melted. Pour over the cookie base and spread evenly. **Be careful—the bowl may be hot!**

Put in the fridge for at least an hour to harden, then cut into squares with a sharp knife. Put the treats on parchment paper in a decorated tin.

Quick Lemon Cookies

You will need:
- ♥ ½ c. (120 mL) butter
- ♥ ½ c. (120 mL) sugar
- ♥ 1½ c. (350 mL) plain flour
- ♥ ¼ tsp (1.25 mL) baking powder
- ♥ 1 egg
- ♥ 1 large lemon
- ♥ pinch of salt
- ♥ sugar for sprinkling

1. Finely grate the lemon **zest**, then squeeze the juice into a bowl.

2. In a large mixing bowl, **beat** the butter and sugar with a wooden spoon until creamy.

This is easier if the butter is soft.

3. Crack in the egg and beat again until light and fluffy.

Pssst... Some ovens cook faster than others, so keep an eye on your cookies and don't let them burn.

4. Stir in the flour, lemon zest and juice, baking powder, and a pinch of salt. Mix to form a ball of dough, then cover the bowl with cling wrap and refrigerate for a couple of hours.

5. Preheat the oven to 400 °F (200 °C). Roll out the dough to ¼ inch (5 mm) thick on a floured surface, sprinkling on extra flour if it's sticky. Cut shapes with cookie cutters.

6. Place the shapes on a baking tray lined with parchment paper and sprinkle with sugar. Bake for about 10 minutes, until the edges of the cookies are light brown.

7. Cool the cookies on a wire rack, then present in a tin or a cellophane bag tied with ribbon.

Try using orange or lime instead of lemon, or adding fresh ginger.

Bath Sets

Soaps, bubble bath, shower gel, and other bath products make lovely presents, but special gift sets are often expensive. It's cheaper—and more personal—to buy items separately and arrange them yourself in a box or basket.

Artsy Soaps

Wrap large soaps in gift wrap, tissue paper, or fabric, or use a scarf as an extra gift. Tie everything with ribbon or lace. You could also try making a fun soap fish!

1. Take a large square of netting and fold it in half.

2. Wrap it around an oval soap and secure with a rubber band.

3. Cover the band with ribbon, and glue on googly eyes or felt circles. Add shiny stickers or sequins and push in colored pins for extra decoration.

Make sure the sharp points of the pins don't stick out of the soap.

Bath Bunnies

A fluffy washcloth is perfect for lining a bath gift basket. You could also turn it into a cute bath bunny and use it to wrap a pretty soap.

Pssst... Spray or drip a little of your favorite perfume into your gift box or basket.

1. Lay the cloth flat and fold in the corner with the label and the opposite corner, like this. Tuck the label under the fold.

2. Roll up one side of the cloth to the middle, keeping it as tight as possible. Do the same on the other side.

3. Fold the cloth in half and place a small soap in the middle. Use a thin rubber band or hair tie to keep the soap in place.

4. Fold up the ends of the cloth to make the head, then tie ribbon around it, leaving the ends sticking up.

Use a band the same color as your cloth, so it doesn't show.

*5. Tweak the ends so they stand up like ears. Glue on mini pom-poms or felt shapes to make a face and fluffy tail, or draw on features with **fabric pens**.*

Bathtime Facts

Traditional Marseille soap blocks have been made for more than 600 years.

Bath bombs contain chemicals that fizz furiously when dropped into water.

A woman named Charlotte Lee has 5,631 rubber ducks, the largest collection in the world!

Fun with Fabric

Materials such as felt, cotton, and wool make beautiful stuffed animals, clothes, and accessories. Don't worry if you're not a sewing expert—there are plenty of great fabric gifts you can create without special skills.

Handy Bags

A bag is a really useful gift, whether it's used for school books, shopping or beach gear. Here are some smart ideas for transforming a plain, reusable cotton bag into a personalized present.

Simple Sewing

Create colorful stripes across the front of your bag using ribbon, lace, and **rickrack**.

Pin each strip in place, then sew across in neat, evenly spaced stitches. Use either a similar color of thread to hide stitches or a contrasting color to make them stand out. Don't forget to remove the pins when you're done!

Stitch in and out, like this. Finish on the inside of the bag and tie a knot.

Buttons and Felt

Add bright buttons by sewing an X through the holes with thick thread. You could also use felt to make shapes or spell names or initials. Remember that sewing becomes trickier farther down the bag (when you're reaching inside) so put most features higher up.

Finishing Touches

Extras such as beads or felt pockets help make your design unique. And if you're feeling generous, pop an extra present inside! How about a book with a sewn felt and ribbon bookmark, or an apron decorated in the same style as the bag?

Some artists make felt by scrunching wool fibers together in soapy water.

Making lace with a needle and thread is an ancient craft that is still practiced today.

Pssst… If you don't feel confident with a needle and thread, buy **fabric glue** instead.

Crocheting involves using a small hook to knit thread or yarn.

Plants and Pots

Many plants are cheap and easy to grow from seed, and they look fantastic displayed in hand-decorated pots. Here are some great ideas for green-thumbed gifts.

Healthy Herbs

The best plants to start with are edible herbs. Not only do they grow quickly, both outdoors or on a windowsill, but they also smell lovely and are useful for adding to stews, pasta sauces, and salads.

Chives

Basil

Coriander

Rosemary

Mint

Plan Your Pot

To save time repotting dainty seedlings, grow your herbs in the pot you'll give them away in. Ordinary pots are very plain, so find a pretty **ceramic** holder in a thrift store, or decorate the pot itself before planting your seeds.

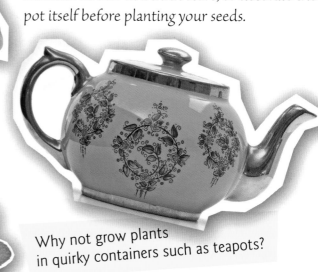

Why not grow plants in quirky containers such as teapots?

Remember to paint the inside, too.

Painting Pots

Acrylic paints are great for decorating plastic or **terracotta** pots. Use a sponge to paint the whole surface evenly, then add details with a thin brush or make prints with bits of sponge.

Pssst... Be careful with acrylic paint as it won't come off clothes once it dries!

Don't forget you'll need a saucer to place the pot on.

EMILY

Plan out a design before you start painting.

Check the seed packet for any extra growing instructions.

Sowing and Growing

Once your pot is ready, fill it with good quality **compost**. Sprinkle a few seeds on the surface, cover with a thin layer of compost, and water well. Leave in a sunny spot, and don't let the soil dry out. Seedlings should sprout in a couple of weeks.

Making Markers

Plant markers are useful for labeling your herbs and listing helpful information. Make colorful markers from popsicle sticks or skewers and paper or felt shapes.

BASIL

MINT

ROSEMARY

It's a Wrap!

Well-wrapped gifts look extra special, so take your time on presentation and try to be neat. Alternatively, use a gift bag and line it with tissue paper. Here are some more tips and ideas.

Reuse and Recycle

You don't need to spend a fortune! Keep old gift bags, tags, and ribbon, and reuse them whenever you can. Simple materials can look more stylish than fussy ones—for example, plain brown parcel paper looks artistic tied up with string, lace, or yarn, perhaps with beads threaded on.

Pssst... Create cute mini envelopes (see pages 14-15) for gift tags.

Wrapping Facts

Extravagant Victorian wrapping paper was so thick that it was hard to fold.

Red is lucky in China, so Chinese gifts are often wrapped in red.

Furoshiki are traditional Japanese cloths used to wrap clothing, presents, or even packed lunches.

Origami Gift Boxes

Make these gift boxes with squares of gift wrap. An 8 inch (20 cm) square makes a 3 inch (7 cm) box; make sure your paper is the right size for your gift.

1. *With the paper square plain side up, fold it in half from top to bottom, then from left to right, and unfold it again.*

2. *Fold each point into the center, using the creases as guides.*

3. *Now fold the bottom and top halves into the center.*

4. *Unfold, then fold in the left and right halves the same way.*

5. *Pull out the top and bottom points, and stand the left and right sides upright to form the sides of the box.*

6. *Push in the corners of the top point, and fold it into the box.*

7. *Do the same with the other point to finish the box.*

8. *Use a square about 1/4 inch (5 mm) bigger to make a lid.*

Abbie

29

Glossary

acrylic paints
Fast-drying paints that can be mixed with water or used straight from the tube. Acrylic paints can't be washed off when dry.

allergy
An extreme sensitivity to something, leading to reactions, such as sneezing and skin rashes, or sometimes even dizziness and difficulty breathing.

beat
To stir or whip ingredients rapidly, adding air to make them light and fluffy.

borders
Colored or decorated strips around the edges of a card.

ceramic
A hard substance, such as pottery or china.

collage
A collection of materials, artistically arranged and glued onto a surface.

compost
A rich, crumbly mixture of rotted plants and other natural matter. Compost contains plenty of nutrients to help seedlings grow.

embossed
Decorated with a raised design.

fabric glue
Glue for sticking fabrics together. Good quality fabric glue won't wash out.

fabric pens
Pens containing permanent ink that is designed not to fade or wash out of fabric.

felt
Fabric made from matted wool. Felt is easy to cut, cheap to buy, and comes in lots of different colors.

intolerance
A bad reaction to certain foods, making the person feel ill.

knead
To press and mold a mixture with your hands to work it into a smooth dough.

mount
To fix or set something in place to display it.

pinking shears
Scissors with serrated blades that cut in a zigzag pattern.

rickrack
Flat, narrow, cotton braid, woven in a wavy, zigzag shape.

terracotta
Hard, orange-brown clay, often made into planting pots.

truffles
Soft, bite-sized sweets, often made from chocolate or cream.

zest
The outer layer of the peel from a lemon, orange, or other citrus fruit. When grating zest, stop when you reach the white layer, as this is very bitter.

Smart Sites

www.enchantedlearning.com/crafts/cards
Lots of effective card-making ideas, including easy pop-up techniques.

www.paper-design.wonderhowto.com/how-to/make-3d-pop-up-card-356460/
How to make a fantastic pop-up card using the flower design on page 9.

www.artistshelpingchildren.org/barsofsoapcraftsideasdecorationskids.html
Inventive ways to turn soaps into all kinds of creative gifts.

www.activityvillage.co.uk/gifts_kids_can_make.htm
Clever craft ideas for all kinds of imaginative homemade gifts.

www.kidspot.com.au/Christmas-Christmas-crafts-Make-your-own-wrapping-paper+3760+117+article.htm
Great suggestions for making your own wrapping paper for Christmas and other occasions.

Index